IMAGES
of America

BARKSDALE AIR FORCE BASE

Lt. Eugene Hoy Barksdale was born in 1897 and died in 1926. (Courtesy Eighth Air Force Museum, Lt. Hoy Barksdale Collection.)

IMAGES
of America

BARKSDALE AIR FORCE BASE

Shawn M. Bohannon, John Andrew Prime,
and H.D. "Buck" Rigg

ARCADIA
PUBLISHING

ISBN 978-0-7385-1428-4

Published by Arcadia Publishing
Charleston, South Carolina

Printed in the United States of America

Library of Congress Catalog Card Number: 2002101536

For all general information contact Arcadia Publishing at:
Telephone 843-853-2070
Fax 843-853-0044
E-mail sales@arcadiapublishing.com
For customer service and orders:
Toll-Free 1-888-313-2665

Visit us on the Internet at www.arcadiapublishing.com

To my parents, John and Nedra Bohannon, for their support and belief in me during the long, and sometimes difficult, road I've traveled on my continuing Air Force journey. To them this work is humbly dedicated.

—Shawn M. Bohannon

To my father, Lt. Col. Stephen W. Prime Sr., who served his country and died at Barksdale; to my mother, Helen Seco Prime, who, like most military spouses, remained the silent, unknown, sustaining hero; and to my wife, Lila, the bravest person I know.

—John Andrew Prime

To my family (the Rigg family and our Air Force family), especially my understanding wife Helen F. Lindsay, our son Trey, and our daughter Lee—all of whom have been touched by our involvement in Barksdale Air Force Base—past and present. Of course, and very importantly, my mother, Gerry, and father, Lt. Col. H.M. "Hal" Rigg (1929–2000), for teaching your four boys the importance of learning to remember and honor the past—and to remember and honor our brave, professional men and women that make up our Armed Forces. Thank you for the privilege of being a member of an Air Force family. What a lifetime of adventures it has been! As Barksdale Air Force Base was your last assignment—ending an illustrious 30 year Air Force career—it was a fitting place to culminate your service to a, more times than not, grateful nation. To this end, I dedicate this book—a small and grateful tribute.

—H. D. "Buck" Rigg

Contents

ACKNOWLEDGMENTS

The authors would like to take this opportunity to acknowledge a representative few of the many people who are dedicated to the preservation of history.

A special thank you to Eric Brock and Clifton Cardin for convincing us to take on this wonderful project. Katie White, thank you for putting up with three of us at once.

Representing the hundreds whose leadership and participation in the stewardship of Barksdale Air Force Base and its legacy have made Barksdale the show base that it is: Overton Brooks, Sen. Russell Long, Sen. J. Bennett Johnston, Sen. Mary Landrieu, U.S. Rep. Jim McCrery, State Rep. Billy Montgomery, Mrs. Helen Black, Mr. Larry Lepinsky, and Mr. Don We[illegible]. Mayors Clyde Fant, Marvin Anding, David Jones, and George Dement; Colonels E.Y. Brown, Ken Patterson, Robert Straughan IV, Al Herring, and Tony Imondi; Generals David Wade, Brett Dula, Russell Dougherty, Richard M. Hoban, David Jones, Richard L. Lawson, Peyt Cote, E.S. Harris, Jr., Robert Herres, Eugene Habiger, J.J. Murphy, William Campbell, Phil Ford, Steve Croker, Ron Marcotte, Tom Keck, Jim Hawkins, Charles Minter, William E. Eubank, Spencer Hardy, Will Fraser, and Curt Bedke—history makers all—and a special thank you to those who provided the documentation on which this book, in great part, is based—the many, often nameless, Army and Air Force photographers and historians and information specialists assigned to Barksdale Field/Air Force Base.

Others who have contributed greatly to our being able to tell this story are the civic leaders and Barksdale support groups that, from the inception of the base and still to this day, champion this national treasure. They are the Shreveport-Bossier City Chambers of Commerce, The Military Affairs Council, their sub-committee on the Eighth Air Force Museum, Barksdale Forward, the Committee of 100, Eighth Air Force Consultation Committee, and Eighth Air Force Museum Association, to name a few. Other contributors include Allan Lazarus, Bill Grabill, Langston McEachern, Grant Hales, Dan Whiteman, Walter Boyne, Peter Merlin, Warren Bodie, Bryan Nicklas, Fred Johnson, Lt. Col. Rod Lees, Ray Knee, Virgil Barnett, Becky Sterba, Robert Haddox, Master Sergeant Billy Gaydon, Gary Mackey, Maj. Joanne Stanton, Robert Langley, Gary Bagshaw, Staff Sergeant Keith Strom, Walt Fortuna, Jim Drudge, Dan Rigg, George Rigg, Art Rigg, Cecil Clevenger, Doug Stump, Wade Meyers, David Miller, Rod Duchesne, Phil Cooper, Rich Masters, George Prince, Henry Goff, Galen Suiter, Joe Jester, Gavin Wilson, Phil Myers, the Lester Thomas family, Capt. Amie Brockway, Capt. Will Manley, Master Sergeant Ken Mattingly, Capt. Denise Kerr, Carla Pampe, Art Nerio, Ron Nelson, Mike Kaplan, Katherine Brash Jeter, Denise Raydor, Derrick Shine, Michael Craft, Judy Pace Christie, Alan English, Craig Durrett, Martha Matlock, and Dot Landry. A very special acknowledgement goes to the Barksdale family, including Shannon Hetter and daughter Megen, Mary Agnes Folsom, Katherine Luftig, Elizabeth MacKay, Dan and Lisa Tyner, Hoy Barksdale Speer, The Honorable Rhesa Barksdale, Jim Barksdale, Thomas Barksdale, Bryan Barksdale, Claiborne Barksdale and the late John Barksdale, and Lura Lee Kelly Genz.

All photographs used in this book are courtesy of the Eighth Air Force Museum except as noted.

INTRODUCTION

It is my hope and that of the authors, that when you finish this book you too will have a greater appreciation for and understanding of Barksdale Air Force Base. We trust you will also further appreciate the role it has played in the development of today's United States Air Force and, more significantly, its role in the preservation and defense of our nation and of a free people everywhere.

I've included in this brief introduction the speech given by the Secretary of War, the Honorable Patrick J. Hurley, in a post-dedication reception at Shreveport's famous Washington-Youree Hotel on February 2, 1933, to the civilian visionaries of the Ark-La-Tex region that made Barksdale AFB possible.

> "Citizens of Shreveport, today you have honored the hallowed memory of a chivalrous knight of the air who gave his life to advance the science of aviation. In conferring the name of Barksdale Field upon this magnificent center of aviation which your enterprise and your patriotism largely made possible, you are handing down to posterity the name of a pioneer in military aviation. His memory still is cherished by his comrades in the air corps. His record of achievement in the service of his country still arouses the admiration and respect of all patriotic Americans.
>
> If he were with us today, nothing would have pleased Lieutenant Barksdale more than to behold the ideal flying conditions of the field that bears his name, the safety and comfort of his fellow pilots in their new home and the modern equipment that they now enjoy. He would rejoice in the realization of every flyer's dream of a great air armada, capable of taking its place in the national defense of his country for which he gave his life. Since the death of Lieutenant Barksdale, aviation has made tremendous strides. Air pilots, many of them trained in the military schools he attended and some of them of his own classmates, now have crossed oceans, circumnavigated the globe and flown in all weather, fair and foul. Thick fog, the nemesis of the World War, largely has been conquered. Army planes now maneuver and are controlled entirely from the air. Mechanical failures have been reduced. Carrying power of planes has been vastly increased. Experiments still continue and no one can foretell with any degree of certainty what aviation still may hold in store for us. We may be certain, however, that in the defense of this country, its air corps will play a dominant role.
>
> Among the pilots of Barksdale field are many who already have made some contribution to the advancement of aviation. From their ranks and from those of their followers may come the future Lindberghs to blaze further trails in the conquest of the air or the future Barksdale to devote their lives to perfect the planes and engines of aviation.
>
> The citizens of Shreveport are fortunate to acquire such a useful and interesting enterprise. The war department is happy to maintain a flying field under such ideal conditions.
>
> Barksdale field is a military establishment. It is a part of the national defense of the United States. Our Government has no imperialistic designs. It desires to live on terms

of peace and amity with all mankind. The American people have no desire to maintain a system of national defense that will become a menace to the peace and happiness of any other people. We will maintain that degree of national defense essential to the liberty of the people and the maintenance of free institutions. I am convinced that adequate national defense is the most effective assurance of peace. Today we dedicate the Barksdale field, not only as an element of our national defense but as a further guarantee of peace."

It is amazing to read from a document that dates nearly 70 years ago and realize how the uttered tributes and possibilities of Barksdale Field have come to pass. For those of us whose good fortune included an assignment or two at Barksdale, this wonderful book is like a visit to an old and respected friend—and one who still reflects a vibrant future. Enjoy.

Brett M. Dula
Lieutenant General, USAF, (Ret.)

One

BARKSDALE—THE MAN
1897–1926

Looking serious and stern, Hoy Barksdale is seen in profile in the cockpit of a Curtiss biplane in 1925 at McCook Field, Ohio. Barksdale was preparing to take the airplane up for a test flight. (Courtesy Eighth Air Force Museum, Lt. Hoy Barksdale Collection.)

The Barksdale family gathers in front of its house at Goshen Springs, Mississippi for this 1902 photo. From left to right, Mattie Taylor, the Barksdale family cook, is seen holding her son, Frank. In the light-colored dress is the family washwoman, Jessie Bryant. Five-year-old Hoy leans against his father, Eugene Sydnor Barksdale. Next to him, in the dark dress, is sister Mary Agnes. Younger brother James is perched against their mother, Kate Williamson Barksdale, with sister Katie Elise leaning on her other side. Sister Clifford Flournoy stands on the end. His second-oldest sister, Sarah Willie, was not present for the impromptu picture taken by an itinerant photographer. Also not visible, though present, was his youngest sibling, Rubie Jeanne, who was born a few months later. Family documents say Hoy's best friend as a youth, and constant fishing companion on the nearby Pearl River, was a young African-American nicknamed "Buck." It is quite likely that "Buck" was Frank Taylor. (Courtesy Eighth Air Force Museum, Lt. Hoy Barksdale Collection.)

Hoy, nine, and his sister Rubie Jeanne, six, pose with fellow students at the one-room Goshen Springs School around 1909. Hoy is at far right, front row, kneeling, while Rubie stands at far right, center row, with her face unfortunately marred by damage to the original photograph. (Courtesy Eighth Air Force Museum, Lt. Hoy Barksdale Collection.)

During his training at Fort Logan H. Roots, Arkansas, Barksdale met fellow officer cadet Ira C. Eaker. At one point in their infantry training, Barksdale met with an Air Service recruiter who stopped at Fort Roots as part of a recruiting jaunt that mixed flying demonstrations with exhortations to the cadets to join the new service. Barksdale, living up to a long family tradition of volunteering, eagerly signed up. Eaker chose to finish the infantry training. Barksdale's route led to the 41st Squadron, Royal Flying Corps for training and combat in World War I. Barksdale's vivid letters convinced Eaker to choose the Air Service over the infantry as his career path. That decision would change the course of United States military aviation. Eaker became one of the architects of strategic bombardment that helped win World War II and has directed air strategy by the United States and other nations to this day. (Courtesy Eighth Air Force Museum, Lt. Hoy Barksdale Collection.)

On leave, just before departing for the front in World War I, Hoy is photographed with his mother and father in Mississippi. The bond between mother and son is evident. This picture was taken in 1917. (Courtesy Eighth Air Force Museum, Lt. Hoy Barksdale Collection.)

In April 1917, Hoy Barksdale joined tens of thousands of other young American men facing the prospect of war overseas. Like most, he was young and did not know what to expect, as shown by this cheerful, youthful study. Note the British-style uniform, leggings, and swagger stick. (Courtesy Eighth Air Force Museum, Lt. Hoy Barksdale Collection.)

Student pilots in Great Britain listen to an instructor in late 1917 or early 1918. Hoy Barksdale is second from the left, front row, staring intently at the lecturer. Barksdale's path led him from Fort Logan H. Roots in Arkansas to basic flight training in Austin, Texas, to Queens Cadet Squadron at Queens College, Oxford, to the Exeter Cadet Squadron, Exeter. By October 1917, Barksdale had survived his first crash—in a Sopwith Pup—but remained six months from his baptism of fire in combat over France. (Courtesy Eighth Air Force Museum, Lt. Hoy Barksdale Collection.)

Hoy Barksdale and other student pilots in an English squadron study a diorama to learn proper airfield procedure in this candid shot taken in late 1917 or very early 1918. The Mississippian is third from right. (Courtesy Eighth Air Force Museum, Lt. Hoy Barksdale Collection.)

Barksdale is second from left, front row, in this view of pilots with the 25th Aero Squadron, Toul, France, in November 1918. By this time, Barksdale was a veteran with three confirmed kills and five ground victories, all earned while flying with the British. He had survived being shot down behind German lines. He used a Very pistol to destroy his airplane lest it fall into German hands and hid in a shell hole until he was rescued the next morning when British troops overran that sector. His service with the American 25th, which lasted all of five days before the Armistice was declared, was peaceful by comparison to his service for the King. (Courtesy Eighth Air Force Museum, Lt. Hoy Barksdale Collection.)

This SE 5 biplane of the 25th Aero Squadron stands ready for its pilot, Hoy Barksdale, and combat, though Barksdale did not encounter the enemy during his service with the unit. His two months at Toul, France, involved routine combat patrols and reconnaissance flights. (Courtesy Eighth Air Force Museum, Lt. Hoy Barksdale Collection.)

After Barksdale returned from Europe in February 1919, he was posted to Mitchel Field, Long Island, where his life and work were profoundly affected during the course of his assignment. He served with the 1st Aero Squadron and is shown in this group photo of pilots middle row, second from left. The social whirl of New York City, with its high society and the American public's fascination with aviation, caused him to grow up quickly. Here he would meet Lura Lee Dunn, the woman who would share the rest of his life. (Courtesy Eighth Air Force Museum, Lt. Hoy Barksdale Collection.)

Hoy Barksdale stands front and center in this lineup of the officers basketball team at Mitchel Field, Long Island. His prewar friend Ira Eaker stands far left. Athletics have always been a vital part of the military lifestyle. Barksdale played on his college basketball and baseball teams and was an avid golfer, so much so that after his death an award was named in his memory. (Courtesy Eighth Air Force Museum, Lt. Hoy Barksdale Collection.)

In 1919, Barksdale met Lura Lee Dunn, who would become his wife two years later. Lura and her parents, Robert and Edna Dunn, lived in New York, but her roots were arguably as Southern as Barksdale's own—Robert Dunn was a native of Little Rock, Arkansas. The Dunns reveled in their Southern heritage and invited Barksdale and other aviators with Southern ties to Hollis House, their luxurious home in Brentwood, Long Island. This view of Hoy and Lura, as well as other photos that show the lanky Barksdale with his peers, explains his nickname "High Pockets." (Courtesy Eighth Air Force Museum, Lura Lee Kelly Genz Collection.)

Most photographs of Hoy Barksdale do not show him smiling, but this view is doubtless one many of his friends carried in their minds long after he died. The cares, worries, and serious side of military life and duty, which often make smiles disappear when cameras come out, are gone in this very candid view of two young people in love. (Courtesy Eighth Air Force Museum, Lura Lee Kelly Genz Collection.)

When an airman puts a woman's name on his airplane, it is as formal a declaration of intent as an engagement notice in the New York Times. Barksdale put Lura Lee's name on his DeHavilland DH-4B, seen here at Mitchel Field around 1921. Note Barksdale's relaxed stance and the empty bomb racks under the port wing. Barksdale used this aircraft in 1920–1921 to establish several aviation records and to take part in the 1921 bombing trials with Gen. Billy Mitchell off the Virginia-North Carolina capes. During the bombing trials, Barksdale met a fellow lieutenant in the air service, Jimmy Doolittle. Doolittle, who would become one of the greatest aviators of the 20th century, had an immense impact on the future career of Barksdale. (Courtesy Eighth Air Force Museum, Lt. Hoy Barksdale Collection.)

In September 1921, air power advocates proved that tiny airplanes could deal deathblows to mighty battleships. Here a DH-4B of the kind Barksdale flew in these trials has dropped a phosphorus bomb on the obsolete battleship USS *Alabama*. The capital ship was sunk in the demonstration. (Courtesy Eighth Air Force Museum, Lt. Hoy Barksdale Collection.)

In 1921, Lura Lee Dunn poses in the gown in which she wed Hoy Barksdale. The two were married that December 15, a Thursday, in an Episcopal service at the Cathedral of the Incarnation, Garden City, Long Island. (Courtesy Eighth Air Force Museum, Lura Lee Kelly Genz Collection.)

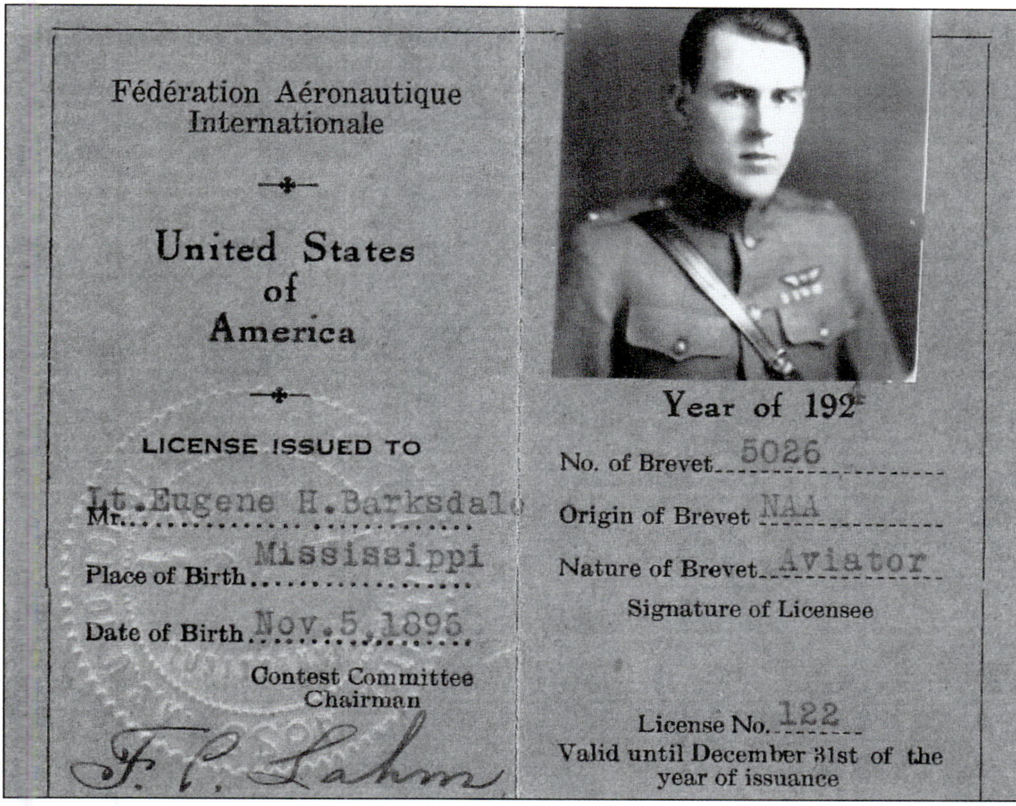

Fédération Aéronautique Internationale

United States of America

LICENSE ISSUED TO

Mr. Lt. Eugene H. Barksdale

Place of Birth Mississippi

Date of Birth Nov. 5, 1895

Contest Committee Chairman

F. P. Lahm

Year of 192

No. of Brevet 5026

Origin of Brevet NAA

Nature of Brevet Aviator

Signature of Licensee

License No. 122

Valid until December 31st of the year of issuance

Hoy Barksdale's pilot license is No. 122, which speaks volumes to people in the brotherhood and sisterhood of flight. The license was signed by Barksdale's former commander in the 25th Aero Squadron, F.P. Lahm. Lahm would eventually rise to the grade of brigadier general and was the first man to be rated as a pilot in United States military service. (Courtesy Eighth Air Force Museum, Lt. Hoy Barksdale Collection.)

This photograph, c. 1924, shows from left to right, Mr. Driggs, Col. Gerald C. Brant, Lieutenant Barksdale, and Lt. Walter Richards relaxing next to Barksdale's DH-4B after a record 90-minute flight from New York to Boston. Notable in the photo with Barksdale is Brant, who would later serve as the second commander of Barksdale Field, 1936–1937. (Courtesy Eighth Air Force Museum, Lt. Hoy Barksdale Collection.)

In November 1923, Barksdale was assigned as a test pilot to the Flight Test Section, Engineering Division, McCook Field, near Dayton, Ohio. He joined the finest pilots then in the United States Air Service, including his old friend Jimmy Doolittle. America's premier test pilots stand in front of a Engineering Division CO-5. They are, from left to right, (front row) civilian pilot R.G. Lockwood, Lt. George Tourtellot, Lt. James H. "Jimmy" Doolittle, and Lt. William N. Amis; (back row) Lt. Harold Johnson, Hoy Barksdale, Lt. John A. Macready, Lt. James T. Hutchinson, Lt. Reuben C. Moffat, and civilian pilot Louis G. Meister. In front of the group are the "Flying Ass" and "Quacking Duck" trophies, presented to fliers who did dumb things while flying. (Courtesy Eighth Air Force Museum, Lt. Hoy Barksdale Collection.)

Hoy Barksdale was an avid sportsman and was acknowledged as one of the finer golfers in military service. Here he is seen at Fort Leavenworth, Kansas, in 1924, taking part in an Army golf tournament. Standing to Barksdale's left is Maj. J.F. Curry, who was the McCook Field commander during Barksdale's service there. (Courtesy Eighth Air Force Museum, Lt. Hoy Barksdale Collection.)

These are the remains of the Douglas O-2 observation plane that crashed just northwest of McCook Field on August 11, 1926, killing Hoy Barksdale. Witnessing the horror were several of his McCook Field peers, as well as Assistant Secretary of War F. Trubee Davison, who would dedicate Barksdale Field in his honor seven years later. (Courtesy Eighth Air Force Museum, Lt. Hoy Barksdale Collection.)

Barksdale's simple stone at Arlington National Cemetery, Washington, bears the year of his death and the year the War Department believed to be of his birth. He was buried five days after his accident, with full military honors. It would be nearly seven years before a greater monument to his memory and his vision would rise from the cotton fields of Northwest Louisiana. (Courtesy Eighth Air Force Museum, Lt. Hoy Barksdale Collection.)

This is Barksdale's last official portrait, taken in 1926. Ironically, just before his death, Barksdale helped scout a location for a military airfield close to his Mississippi roots. He flew as far west as Monroe, Louisiana. (Courtesy Eighth Air Force Museum, Lt. Hoy Barksdale Collection.)

Two

From Cotton Fields to an Air Field 1924–1932

Several three-mule-team plows were used to till under hundreds of acres of cotton to provide the planting of a new crop—concrete. Thousands of cubic yards of concrete and several tons of steel replaced woods and fields, out of which grew what some called a "little French Village." Barksdale Field proved better than any cash crop. By the end of its sixth decade, the base had an annual economic impact measured in the hundreds of millions of dollars.

Shreveport businessman and Air Service Reserve Capt. Conway Allen thought Shreveport would be a splendid location for an army airfield. The United States Army's Fourth Corps area, the Southeastern United States, had fewer strategically placed airfields than other districts. Allen thought that placing such a field near Shreveport would greatly remedy that deficiency. Allen gathered a group of local business and civic leaders to form an aeronautical committee to select a location for the field.

Seen almost due west across Shreveport from Bossier City, Cross Lake commands the top of this picture. An area south of the lake, which is Lakeview Subdivision, was the committee's first choice for the airfield. An army advance team that scouted the location would disagree.

John D. Ewing, a Captain in the Air Service, led a public drive to create Cross Lake in the mid-1920s and was adept at stoking the fires of public opinion. As editor and publisher of the *Shreveport Times*, he also enjoyed a public forum that allowed acquisition of the airfield to become a local priority. As one of the powers that molded editorial and local opinion, Ewing was a leader in the drive to present the airfield as an economic stimulus and to justify a public bond issue to purchase land for the airfield.

Retired United States Army Col. Dan W. Spurlock, a Standard Oil executive and commander of Lowe-McFarlane American Legion Post 14, was on the aeronautical committee. He tirelessly wrote letters and sent telegrams to politicians and army officials, including Brig. Gen. Billy Mitchell, promoting the notion of an airfield in Northwest Louisiana.

Retired United States Army Col. John Tucker, a prominent Shreveport attorney, was chosen to handle the many complex legal issues that proponents of the army airfield knew would arise. The acquisition of any tract of land large enough for air operations would require title searches on hundreds of smallholdings, with some tracts handed down through generations of heirs of large plantations.

United States Army Air Corps Reserve Capt. Harold Ross Harris, in civilian life a crop duster, was hired by the aeronautical committee to scout a location he thought better suited to the Air Corps needs. He was a test pilot at McCook Field with Hoy Barksdale and Jimmy Doolittle. (Courtesy Eighth Air Force Museum, Lt. Hoy Barksdale Collection.)

Harris finally decided that this land was best suited for an airfield. The best location wound up containing some of the best farmland in Bossier Parish, land held by more than 800 owners. This view, looking south over what is now Interstate 20, shows the rich alluvial cotton fields and pecan groves that awaited the lawyers, surveyors, and teams of brawny laborers who would transform it.

Lt. George A. McHenry, Lt. Col. H.C. Pratt, Col. W.H. Noble, and Maj. John B. Brooks made up the army survey board that inspected the site selected by Harris. They approved his choice over the one the aeronautical committee had selected. This forced Shreveport to begin the delicate process of acquiring land in a different parish. Special legislation had to be pushed through the Louisiana legislature to make this happen. It required the cooperation of Louisiana Gov. Huey P. Long, a former Shreveporter and master of political intrigue who did not always see eye-to-eye with the members of the aeronautical committee.

On November 7, 1930, the great moment finally arrived. Shreveport civic leaders signed the deed papers that conveyed 22,000 acres of Bossier Parish land to the federal government for use as an air-bombing and gunnery range. Pictured here are (seated) John D. Ewing (chairman of the 3rd Attack Wing Committee), Shreveport Mayor L.E. Thomas, and Andrew Querbes Sr. (chairman of the General Citizens Committee); (standing) Randle T. Moore, E.A. Gillespie, United States Attorney Phillip H. Mecom, Shreveport Chamber of Commerce immediate past President Yandell Boatner, historian and Assistant United States Attorney J. Fair Hardin, United States Rep. John N. Sandlin, City Attorney B.F. Roberts, Chamber of Commerce Secretary-manager C.W. Longwill, attorney John H. Tucker (vice chairman of the 3rd Attack Wing Committee), City Engineer H. Earl Barnes, attorney Sam W. Mason, Chamber of Commerce President B.H. Bolinger, and Parish Assessor A.G. Hammett.

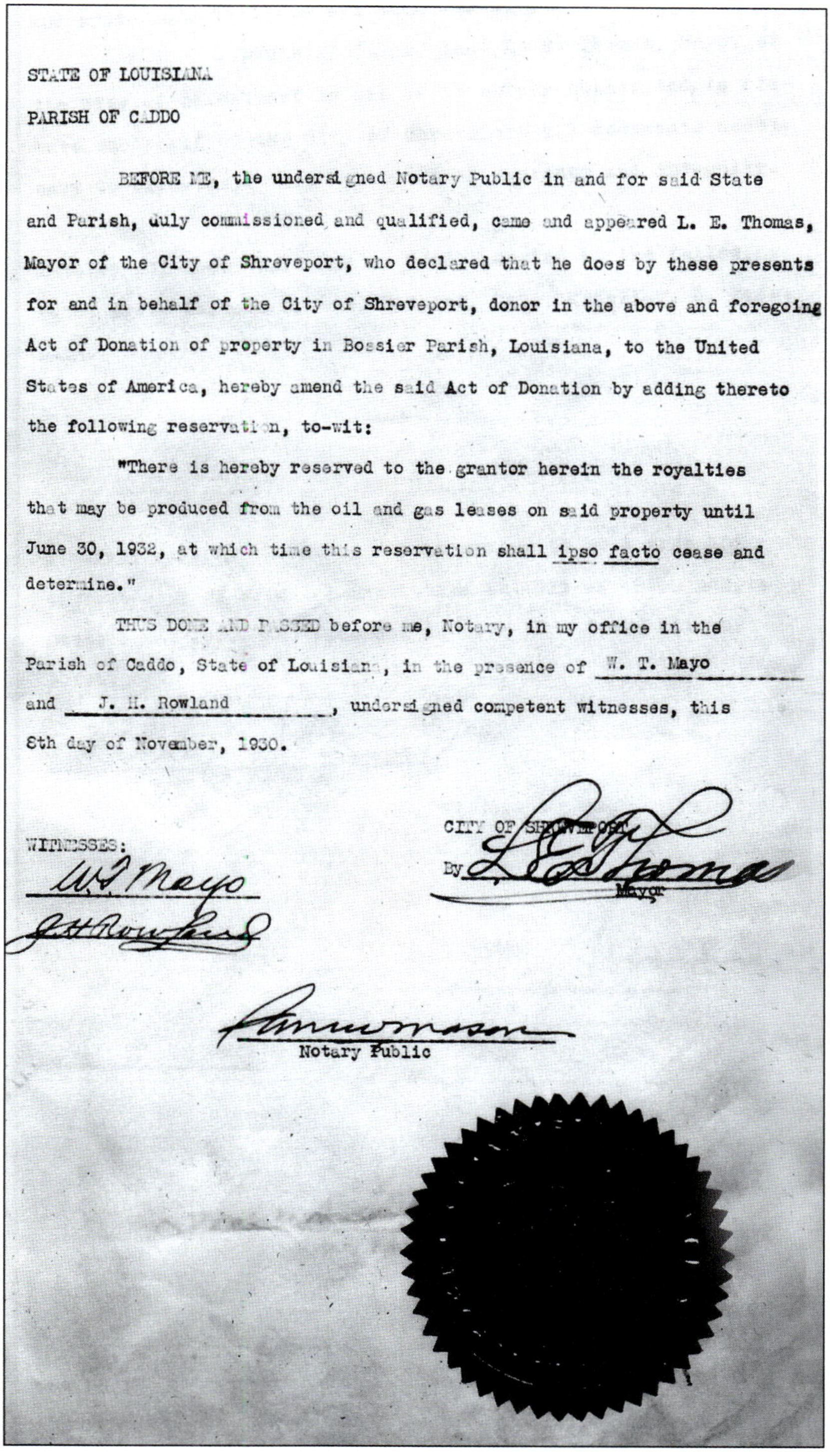

STATE OF LOUISIANA

PARISH OF CADDO

BEFORE ME, the undersigned Notary Public in and for said State and Parish, duly commissioned and qualified, came and appeared L. E. Thomas, Mayor of the City of Shreveport, who declared that he does by these presents for and in behalf of the City of Shreveport, donor in the above and foregoing Act of Donation of property in Bossier Parish, Louisiana, to the United States of America, hereby amend the said Act of Donation by adding thereto the following reservation, to-wit:

"There is hereby reserved to the grantor herein the royalties that may be produced from the oil and gas leases on said property until June 30, 1932, at which time this reservation shall *ipso facto* cease and determine."

THUS DONE AND PASSED before me, Notary, in my office in the Parish of Caddo, State of Louisiana, in the presence of W. T. Mayo and J. H. Rowland, undersigned competent witnesses, this 8th day of November, 1930.

WITNESSES:

W. T. Mayo

J. H. Rowland

CITY OF SHREVEPORT

By L. E. Thomas

Mayor

Notary Public

A day after the deed was signed, the above amendment was signed to allow revenues from oil and gas leases on the donated reservation to continue coming to the Aeronautical Committee until the planned arrival of the Field's First Flying Unit expected in mid-1932.

Within weeks, teams of men and mules were on the land. The first $50,000 allocation from the War Department was to turn under the existing cotton fields and replace them with Bermuda grass, on which would slowly emerge the runways, buildings, and roads of Barksdale Field.

This 1931 aerial view of Barksdale Field, seen from above the Red River, already shows the Parisian axial layout for what would become grand boulevards. Foundations for non-commissioned officer quarters and barracks and warehouses are springing up in the southwest quadrant and along the grass runway. The foundations of future officers quarters can be seen north of the main east-west boulevard.

Another 1931 aerial view, looking north across the field, shows the first buildings at Barksdale rising from their foundations. These are the quartermaster warehouses, through which all the construction materials, tools, heavy equipment, and supplies would be channeled.

Two years into the Great Depression and desperate for work, local contract laborers put their shoulders into the hard, dirty job of pouring concrete for Barksdale's future housing foundations. A motorized cement mixer made the work easier than it could have been, but much of the labor was provided by men and animals.

A laborer performs a "slump test," which would show whether freshly mixed concrete had the proper consistency for its intended use.

Later in 1931, homes for company and field-grade officers are rising. The closest house, now 101 Orville Wright Road, was first used by bachelor officers before a purpose-built facility was available. One of this building's first occupants was Lt. Ernest E. Holtzer II, who would be the field's second flying casualty in a 1933 crash.

Workmen on scaffolds install copper gutters on two-story company-grade officer's quarters in 1931. Others mix concrete and stucco for the exteriors of large, roomy accommodations laid out in an aesthetically pleasing manner that still exists today. The houses were designed in French Colonial Revival style, more in keeping with the ambience of Acadian Louisiana.

Houses and offices on Barksdale were built using hollow masonry blocks that provided light, fireproof structures with little or no internal steel. Only roofs were built using wood, allowing the structures to rise quickly from the ashes following fires in the decades to come.

Barksdale witnesses its first hangars being erected along Hangar Line Road and the flight line area. By this time, enlisted housing is well along, and the base has begun to acquire a permanent population.

Another 1931 aerial view shows foundations being poured for the base headquarters building and landmark water tower. At this time, enlisted housing is largely finished, the roomy structures standing like playing pieces on a game board.

The year 1932 sees Barksdale with complete hangars and base operations buildings along its flight line. The first series of barracks is also complete. Hangar roofs are painted in a highly visible yellow-and-black checkerboard pattern common to military airfields at the time. Construction in the middle ground is for the joint military police and firehouse facility.

Looking north: Barksdale Field begins to look like a community in early 1932 as it prepares to welcome its first flying unit, the 20th Pursuit Group, which arrived in October. Maj. Millard F. Harmon and an advance team arrived in July to set up headquarters. The smoke in the center of the cantonment is from the men working on the base standpipe or water tower.

The base standpipe and flagpole are the highest structures in this mid-1932 picture. The completed base headquarters building, barracks, and enlisted housing are ready for occupancy.

With completion of its standpipe and headquarters, Barksdale Field is ready for business in mid-1932. Some were already calling it the "Little French Village." In the span of less than two years, determination and the labor of thousands had turned cotton fields into an airfield.

Three

The Pursuit Years 1932–1935

Ready to welcome visitors and service personnel, the spare and simple West Gate stands in isolation in this 1932 view.

Pictured here is Barksdale Field's first commander, Maj. Millard F. Harmon. Known as "Miff," he was at Barksdale from 1932 to 1936 as commander of the 20th Pursuit Group. He eventually rose to the grade of lieutenant general. The B-17 in which he was a passenger was lost over the Pacific Ocean in March 1945. (Courtesy Eighth Air Force Museum, Helen Harmon Nazzaro Collection.)

One of the many benefits of being assigned to Barksdale Field was the opportunity to commune with nature on its vast reservation. As seen in this photograph, the "First Family of Barksdale" enjoys horseback riding and no doubt, when time permitted, they took in some hunting and fishing, too. Maj. Millard F. "Miff" Harmon is on his horse Rosita, and daughter Helen is on the horse Bo Peep. Wife Alberta and son Buddy are in front, with family dogs, left to right, Cloudy, Mike, Flyer, and Billy. (Courtesy Eighth Air Force Museum, Helen Harmon Nazzaro Collection.)

On November 20, 1932, Barksdale welcomed visitors for the first time. The occupants of the parked cars left them in search of a more advantageous location to watch an aerial review by the 20th Pursuit Group.

Barksdale's first flying casualty was Lt. Brittain Purser. The Louisiana native, from Amite, died December 3, 1932. In his honor, Harmon named two grassy playgrounds near the field grade officer housing "Purser Park." (Courtesy Eighth Air Force Museum, Paul E. Purser Collection.)

Pilots of the 20th Pursuit Group stand before their P-12 fighters, lined up in an early 1933 photo. The hangars in the background remain in service today.

Here are 3rd Attack Group commander Col. Horace Hickham, Assistant Secretary of War F. Trubee Davison, Maj. Millard F. Harmon, and *Shreveport Times* editor-publisher John D. Ewing standing in front of the Wing Operations Building on February 2, 1933. Three of these men would die in airplanes: Hickham in a November 5, 1934 crash at Fort Crockett, Galveston, Texas; Harmon over the South Pacific in 1945; and Ewing of a heart attack in his plane "Newsboy" in 1952. (Courtesy Eighth Air Force Museum, Helen Harmon Nazzaro Collection.)

Dedication Exercises

Barksdale Field

February 2, 1933

Two o'clock

This is the program for Barksdale Field's dedication ceremony on February 2, 1933.

This photo, taken on February 2, 1933, is looking south over the crowd from the field operations and control tower. A crowd of 50,000 to 60,000 people attended.

Two enlisted members of the 77th Pursuit Squadron pose in front of the unit's P-12s at Barksdale Field's dedication day, February 2, 1933. (Courtesy Eighth Air Force Museum, Joe Eddy Maxwell Collection.)

Alberta Harmon, wife of base commander Maj. Millard F. Harmon, seems pleased with the way things are going on dedication day—look at the smile on her face as she wheels to face the camera. (Courtesy Eighth Air Force Museum, Helen Harmon Nazzaro Collection.)

The Distinguished Visitors Area held dignitaries from both the Shreveport area and from Washington, D.C. In the background, military personnel prepare for a pass in review. This photo was taken on February 2, 1933.

Assistant Secretary of War F. Trubee Davison addresses the crowd at Barksdale Field's dedication, February 2, 1933. The whereabouts of the large portrait of Lt. Eugene Hoy Barksdale are unknown today.

The Art Deco Wing Operations Control Tower is the backdrop to a dais on which are seated 3rd Attack Group commander Col. Horace Hickham, Army Air Corps chief Maj. Gen. Benjamin Foulois, and Assistant Secretary of War F. Trubee Davison.

Pilots of the 20th Pursuit Group march to their P-12 fighters to begin their aerial review.

Three local girls walk down a railroad right-of-way on what became Hangar Line Road and is now Lindbergh Road, February 2, 1933. They are going to join the crowd in front of the Wing Operations building and Control Tower. P-12s fly in formation behind them. (Courtesy Eighth Air Force Museum, Maj. B. Hunter Graham Collection.)

Randolph Field flying cadets in Douglas BT-2C basic trainers pass en masse for the review. This was taken on Barksdale Field's dedication day, February 2, 1933.

Another group passes for the review while substantial Keystone bombers approach from the north. Echelons of P-12s and Curtiss P-3s are in the background ready for a dash across the field. The light-colored area is a plowed field, not the sod runway.

Post-dedication ceremonies were at Shreveport's swank Washington-Youree Hotel and at Brookwood, the family mansion of oilman and Barksdale booster James E. Smitherman. Pictured, from left to right, in front of Brookwood, are Assistant Secretary of War F. Trubee Davison, Secretary of War and later ambassador to China Patrick J. Hurley (who was delayed and missed the dedication ceremony), Assistant United States Attorney Seth W. Richardson, and Air Corps chief Maj. Gen. Benjamin Foulois.

Lt. Ernest E. Holtzen II, Barksdale Field's second flying casualty, was killed on December [illegible], 1933 when his P-12 aircraft crashed after being struck by another fighter at an altitude of about 4,500 feet. Flying was a decidedly dangerous profession, as the aviators at Barksdale—and the people of Shreveport and Bossier City—would learn. The Barksdale Bachelor Officers Quarters (BOQ) was dedicated as Holtzen Hall in 1934 to honor this young bachelor.

Barksdale Field's standpipe, now complete and sporting a high-visibility, black-and-yellow checkerboard pattern, casts a long, late-afternoon shadow in this early 1933 view. To the north of the standpipe and base headquarters one can see grading and site preparation for the base hospital and barracks for the 3rd Attack Group.

A torrent courses down Davis Avenue, Barksdale's main north-south avenue, after a thunderstorm in 1933. The prime farmland that became Barksdale was prime floodplain as well, and flash floods continued to be a problem for the streets and ramps on the base for many decades.

The Barksdale Officers Club was dedicated as Patrick Hall in 1934 to the memory of the victim of Barksdale's third fatal air accident, which claimed the life of 1st Lt. Frederick I. Patrick on February 22, 1934. Patrick was the 20th Pursuit Group's Operations officer and was stationed at Barksdale for less than a year when he met his early death in a forced landing at Denison, Texas.

This is the interior of Patrick Hall at Barksdale Officers Club, 1934. A portrait of Lieutenant Patrick hangs above the fireplace. This area is now the main dining area for lunch and evening meals. A life-size oil painting of Lieutenant Barksdale now hangs in the place of Patrick's portrait.

Saplings in the foreground promise greenery later on, but this 1934 view still shows Barksdale Field with an almost surreal Art Deco cleanliness and simplicity. The new base hospital, to the north of the headquarters building and standpipe, is finished and open.

Just before the arrival of the 3rd Attack Group, one of the A-12 *Shrike* attack planes flies over Barksdale Field for an inspection in mid-1934. The group's hangars are under construction in the background just north of the existing hangars.

It was reasonable that in the heart of the stately and elegant structures that made up Barksdale Field it would be a matter of time before the sore-thumb-looking standpipe was covered in complementary French Colonial Revival masonry. This was accomplished in the winter of 1934. The towering icon continues to stand out as the prominent feature and landmark of Barksdale. The standpipe, now referred to as the water tower, is still in use.

Four

The Attack Era
1935–1940

In just two years, the dusty path into Barksdale had turned into a smartly paved road, with brisk traffic and an unbroken horizon of buildings beyond. A fence and a traffic arm signify increased security concerns in this photograph taken of the West Gate in 1935.

The 3rd Attack Group's primary aircraft was the Curtiss A-12 *Shrike II*. This example belongs to the 13th Attack Squadron, whose symbol on the side of the craft shows a skeleton brandishing a blood-tipped scythe.

An echelon formation of A-12 *Shrike II*s flies by in a salute to the 3rd Attack Group's new home in early 1935.

Not men from Mars, but high-fliers of the 20th Pursuit Group wearing early high-altitude gear, including full-faced, leather oxygen masks and standing in front of a Boeing P-26 *Peashooter*.

Members of the Barksdale Field fire brigade pose on their pumper, 1935.

In 1935, Barksdale Field joined Shreveport in its centennial celebration. For that milestone, base personnel created four floats. Each depicted a century's worth of aviation history, detailing man's quest for the sky from mythology to the modern era. Marilyn Lovell, daughter of a Lieutenant Colonel Lovell stationed at the field, poses on the float.

A Goodyear TC-13 blimp makes a refueling stop at Barksdale Field in the middle of a 1937 cross-country flight. An obsolete Keystone B-6A bomber, in the foreground, sits awaiting its fate as a target on the Barksdale bombing range.

By 1937, the Curtiss A-12 *Shrike II* was slowly being phased out and would be replaced by the Northrop A-17. This 3rd Attack Group example is in flight over Barksdale.

Curtiss P-36 *Hawk* fighters of the 20th Pursuit Group are lined up on the ramp for a monthly review by leadership. Pilots stood on the port side of the fuselage in front of the plane's wing while members of the ground crews stood to starboard as officers walked by.

In July 1937, members of the 8th Attack Squadron stand at attention in front of an upgraded Northrop A-17A. In the front row, fourth from the right, is Aviation Cadet William E. Eubank Jr. He would rise to the grade of major general and would fly the first B-52 bomber into United States Air Force service in June 1955.

Here is an aerial view of the awards presentation of the Luke Trophy in July 1937. The Luke Trophy was awarded to the unit with the top gunnery score in the U.S. Army Air Corps. The large plane at center is the Y1B-17, serial number 36-158 of the 49th Bomb Squadron, which was flown to Barksdale from Langley Field, Virginia, home of the 2d Bomb Group. Notice the welcome painted on top of the hangar, center.

The sad demise of a bomber—Keystone B-6 *Panther* meets an unwarrior-like fate as a target on the Barksdale bombing range in 1937.

By 1938, the 3rd Attack Group was renamed the 3rd Bombardment Group and had swapped its attack planes for Martin B-10 bombers. For most of the 1930s, the word Martin was almost synonymous with "bomber," until Boeing took that crown away. Variants of these Martin bombers would remain at Barksdale through early 1942.

In the late 1930s, Barksdale personnel enjoyed a skeet range near the North Gate. It was more than recreation—their skills as gunners depended on frequent opportunities to hone eye-hand coordination. A B-47 *Stratojet* bomber now perches here near the Eighth Air Force Museum. (Eighth Air Force Museum, Dominick Giantonio [a Survivor of the Bataan Death March] Collection.)

This Fokker Y1C-15 ambulance plane was assigned to Barksdale in 1937. The one-of-a-kind aircraft was at Barksdale until 1938 and was used to transport critical care patients to and from the base.

This 1937 postcard shows what may have been one of the shortest-lived curiosities at Barksdale—neon lighting atop the standpipe. The gaudy but memorable apparition was visible for miles. The lights were, naturally, red, white, and blue.

In 1938, an open-air theater occupied green space near the 20th Pursuit Group barracks. The theater is long gone, replaced by a parking lot, and the barracks was later used as 2d Bomb Wing headquarters and then as headquarters for the 2d Support Group. The theater was a solution to the problem of gathering people in scratchy wool uniforms in assembly in summer heat—before air-conditioning.

April 6, 1938, marked the 21st anniversary of the United States' entry into World War I. It was observed as Armed Forces Day with an open house at Barksdale Field. The event was low-key. According to the *Shreveport Times* story welcoming the public, the event was planned "to please the public without actually staging any spectacular air displays." It wrapped up with a barbecue for reserve officers, mostly "Great War" veterans at Shreveport's Forty & Eight Club on Cross Lake.

Pvt. Dean Chastain is seen on duty in the control tower atop the 3rd Wing operations building in this 1938 snapshot. (Courtesy Eighth Air Force Museum, Dean Chastain Collection.)

The fast, sleek Curtiss Y1A-18 *Shrike IIIs* of the 8th Attack Squadron streak over the enlisted quarters of Barksdale Field in 1938. There were only a dozen of these airplanes in service—and nearly half of them are seen in this picture. Barksdale was their first home for in-service testing.

Douglas "Wrong Way" Corrigan visited Shreveport on August 24, 1938, barely a month after he caught the nation's fancy by "accidentally" crossing the Atlantic Ocean when he filed a flight plan for a trip from Brooklyn to California. People then and now debate how one can mess up as badly as he did, and the most charitable theories surmise he deliberately thumbed his nose at authority. But everyday people loved the brash, bantam-sized flier, and Shreveport proved no exception when he toured the nation shortly after his goofy flight. He was treated to a parade through the city and a tour of Barksdale Field. Corrigan later played himself in the movie *The Flying Irishman*. He died in late 1995 at age 88.

In the winter of 1938, a rare blanket of snow carpets Barksdale Field and the Ark-La-Tex, as residents of the confluence of Louisiana, Texas, and Arkansas call the region. The strange wet white carpet sets out in stark relief the tableaux of roads, buildings, and open grassy areas and shows the symmetry and vision of the field's designers.

Southern boys know how to "do snow." Members of the 20th Pursuit Group take full advantage of the white stuff for winter training. Their barracks in the background would later serve as the headquarters of the Eighth Air Force after it moved to the base in the 1970s.

The snow of 1938 provided the proper setting for a Christmas feast. Here, the table is set for members of the 3rd Attack Group in a barracks mess hall.

It is hard to believe that the Douglas B-18 *Bolo* bomber was a serious competitor to the legendary Boeing B-17. In 1939, when these 90th Bomb Squadron airframes arrived to join the 3rd Bombardment Group, the *Bolo* was the successor to the famed Martin that ruled the 1930s, but the four-engine Boeing had yet to prove itself. When a school for bombardiers was established the following year, *Bolos* were used to train the students.

Many fliers are great believers in luck and deity. A post chapel was built and dedicated in 1939, just in time for a flood of weddings that occurred as the nation plunged into war. It was known as, and remains today, simply Chapel 1.

This is an interior view of Chapel 1 taken in 1939. These hallowed walls have witnessed hundreds of christenings, marriages, and wakes for more than 60 years.

Temporary barracks of the 27th Bombardment Group dominate an area that would later become a vast parking lot. The barracks seen in this 1939 photograph would not be demolished until well after World War II. The Douglas B-18 bombers on the flight line belong to the 3rd Bombardment Group.

This 1940 image is of a Douglas A-24 *Dauntless* of the 27th Bomb Group at Barksdale Field. Planes and personnel of this unit, including William E. Eubank Jr., were shipped to the Philippine Islands just as the Japanese attacked in December 1941. The planes were diverted en route, but the personnel continued on to the Philippines, where they served as infantry. The ground crews that stayed to fight the Japanese were captured and were part of the infamous Bataan Death March.

Five

World War II and the Training Era 1940–1949

As Barksdale Field would play an important role in World War II, the familiar arched colonnades around the West Gate Guard house were filled in to provide wartime protection against potential threats.

The original evergreen shrubs and cypress trees planted in 1932 began to overtake the base headquarters building, visible in this 1940 photograph. In 1941, the evergreens were trimmed back and live oaks were planted around the facility.

During the summer months, being on duty at Barksdale was like being in the tropics. Air Force Military policemen can be seen guarding the north gate, dressed in the army tropical uniform. The military police are distinguished by their white spats and white pith helmets. Only a few specialized organizations in the army were authorized this type of gear.

Barksdale was home to the United States Air Corps Bombardier School from 1940 to 1941. In this photograph, aviation cadets from Bombardier Class 41-2 gather before graduation. Of note is cadet Kermit Beahan in the front row, center. Beahan was the bombardier on the B-29 "Bocks Car" whose lethal atomic payload was dropped on Nagasaki, Japan, August 9, 1945, ending World War II. (Courtesy Eighth Air Force Museum, Lt. Col. Lonnie Crook Collection.)

During World War II, Barksdale Field was also home to the Army Air Forces Military Police Training Center. Part of the multifaceted curriculum was airfield defense. To simulate an attack on an airfield, a B-26 Martin *Marauder* "cuts the grass" while laying a thick blanket of tear-gas over the training area. A military police candidate hustles to reach his gas mask.

The vast acreage that made up Barksdale Field provided military police trainees an opportunity to experience realistic scenarios for both European and Pacific theater operations. In this photograph, the day's lesson is about the protection and handling of prisoners of war while in the Pacific Theater.

The first B-24 unit, the 44th Bombardment Group, was established at Barksdale Field just months after the attack on Pearl Harbor. The 44th would create and train America's most famous B-24 organizations, including itself. The 90th, the 93rd, and the 98th Bomb Groups would all go on to be some of the most decorated "Liberator" groups in the Air Force. During World War II, a part of everyday training would have to account for accidents. This incident has a B-24D coming to a stop after the collapse of its nose gear on July 7, 1942.

A 335th Bomb Group Martin B-26 *Marauder* shares a similar indignity as the B-24 when its nose gear collapses. The two incidents occurred on the same day, July 7, 1942. Similar occurrences throughout the war gave rise to the slogan "Two a day, the Barksdale way."

A major, and necessary, change came to the Wing Operations building, specifically Hangar 9, when the familiar large, white letters painted on the roof, proclaiming "BARKSDALE" on the west half and "VISITING SHIPS, ALT 165" on the east half were removed. This was done so the airfield would not be recognized by spies or enemy bombers flying over the area. The words were repainted after the end of hostilities.

A group of young, determined, and apprehensive-looking second lieutenants poses for this 1944 photograph. The "butter bar" lieutenants are members of the Barksdale-based Army Air Forces Chemical Warfare Training Center.

Throughout World War II, morale and recreation events were important activities for service members. Various morale forums provided an opportunity to recharge and forget about the war for a short time. Barksdale Field Services Squadron provided a variety of nightly camp shows, like the USO, Camel Caravan, or entertainment from the local Shreveport-Bossier City schools and churches. All of the entertainment was held at Hangar 9. A favorite activity was the Military Maid Ball, a semi-formal dance allowing the service members to meet and socialize with single young women from the area. Many wartime proposals were initiated by these morale-boosting activities.

When Sgt. Joe "The Brown Bomber" Louis paid Barksdale Field a visit in 1944, the event was a well-received morale boost for all the men. A special exhibition bout was fought in Hangar 9. Sergeant Louis toured the base and met the personnel. In this photograph, Col. William Wright, Barksdale's base commander, is second from the left, next to the Brown Bomber, who is dressed in a satin robe.

Morale activities also took place in this facility—the base movie theater. Originally constructed as the base gym in 1932, the building was converted to a theater in the mid-1930s. The right side of the theater housed the service club, which was also called "The Plantation Room" because a large mural of a southern plantation was painted on an interior wall. The service club also held the base library and technical library.

Several celebrities visited Barksdale throughout World War II. In this 1944 photograph, Hollywood actress Irene Manning is perched in the midst of air and ground crews on the Barksdale ramp. A 335th Bomb Group Martin B-26 serves as an appropriate backdrop. Manning's wartime movies included *Yankee Doodle Dandy*, *The Doughgirls*, and *Hollywood Canteen*.

Since injured soldiers were unable to attend the morale-boosting activities, the entertainment was brought to them. A crowd of patients from the base hospital soaks up the sunshine and the dance exhibition performed by a couple from the Camel Caravan camp show.

A great war hero, Col. John Riley "Killer" Kane, came to Barksdale to bestow awards on fellow aviators. Kane, whose family lived in Shreveport before the war, served at Barksdale Field in the 1930s and would go on to earn the Medal of Honor for the raid against oil refineries at Ploesti, Romania.

About 60 combat crews were trained every month during the war and the success or failure of the training could hinge on the reliability of the aircraft. Maintenance is instrumental in ensuring that trainees have the best possible flying machines available. In the 1944 photograph, women of the Barksdale Sub-Depot are seen working on a Martin B-26.

The "Ditching Pool" was an innovative creation by instructors of the Barksdale survival school. A large, round hole was excavated and a war-weary B-26 hulk was placed in the middle of the hole, which was then filled with water. Combat crews were placed in their crew positions to practice water ditching and egress procedures in a realistic simulation. The ditching pond is long gone—in the mid-1950s, the base Field Training facility was constructed on the site. Today, the Eighth Air Force Museum is in its place.

In 1944, Barksdale Field provided training for the Free French Air Force. The French tri-color flew over Barksdale every Friday while the French trained.

Two members of the French Air Force pose in front of their tarpaper barracks in this 1944 photograph. Several hundred French airmen completed their combat crew training in the Martin B-26.

The participation of all able-bodied persons in various war jobs played a large part in winning the war. One such wartime career was in the Women's Army Corps (WAC). This photograph shows a special display in a downtown Shreveport business showing how local women could join the WACs and work at Barksdale Field in up to 44 different jobs. A "WAC Shack" was set up on the lawn of the Shreveport courthouse to sign up citizens who wanted to work at Barksdale.

In this 1943 photograph, unidentified Barksdale soldiers toil in what was billed as the world's largest Army Victory Garden. By 1945, most of the work was done by German prisoners of war brought in from a POW camp at Ruston. The work was physically demanding, but many were used to this kind of labor before the war. Many former German POWs have visited North Louisiana in the decades since, and some have become United States citizens.

Walking and bicycling were the main forms of transportation around Barksdale Field. Because cars were in short supply, Barksdale came up with a transportation system based on the San Francisco trolleys. Using an old aircraft tug and a specially built trailer, this slow-moving train followed a circuit around the airfield and administrative areas allowing people to get on and off as it went by. It was dubbed the "Toonerville Trolley."

In January 1945, a fire destroyed Barksdale's first two hangars as well as two B-26 bombers that were housed inside. The fire was attributed to a faulty space heater. The steel tracks on which the hangar doors traveled are all that is left of the site today, which was transformed into a parking lot.

German prisoners of war tending the roads and performing grounds maintenance were an unusual sight. In this 1945 photograph, POWs are seen raking grass clippings near the enlisted quarters. (Courtesy Eighth Air Force Museum, Lt. Col. Chuck Gillis Collection.)

On June 9, 1945, Crown Prince Abdul Ilah (third from right), the Regent of Iraq, visited Barksdale Field while touring the United States to inspect American methods of irrigation and reforestation. During his brief visit, the Crown Prince toured the airfield, inspected a B-29 bomber—probably the one seen in the background—and breakfasted at the Officers Club. Col. William B. Wright Jr., commander of Barksdale Field, stands on his left. In April 1939, the Crown Prince assumed the mantle of Regent to his three-year-old nephew, the newly crowned King Faisal II of Iraq. The Crown Prince continued to rule Iraq as regent until the King reached his majority in 1953. On July 14, 1958, the Iraqi monarchy came to a violent end when army officers led by Brig. Abdul Karim Kassem assassinated King Faisal II and Crown Prince Abdul Ilah and declared Iraq a republic. (Courtesy 2d Bomb Wing History Office.)

In May 1945, Barksdale Field celebrated victory in Europe in grand style. Speeches, marching bands, and parading soldiers proclaimed the resolve to end the hostilities still raging in the Pacific Theater.

After World War II Barksdale Field did not slow down its pace as a training center. By 1946, Barksdale became the home of the Air Training Command. Barksdale was the center of all Air Force training activities in the United States until 1949 when the major command moved to Randolph Air Force Base in Texas. At Barksdale, it was replaced by Headquarters Second Air Force under Strategic Air Command.

On September 18, 1947, the United States Air Force (USAF) was born. The first class of multi-engine pilots in the Air Force, Class-47C, graduated from Barksdale Air Force Base. The Barksdale multi-engine class consisted of 50 B-17s, one of which is seen behind the first graduating class of the new USAF. (Courtesy Eighth Air Force Museum, Jim Larkin Collection.)

Snow is always a curiosity at Barksdale and is fairly well documented. In this 1948 photograph, a thick blanket of snow covers the air base. In the foreground is headquarters Air Training Command. On the ramp to the upper left are some of the 50 B-17s and 60 B-25s assigned to the multi-engine and twin-engine school.

Six

PEACE IS OUR PROFESSION 1949–1992

In this 1964 photograph, the West Gate at Barksdale Air Force Base boasts a new sign that reads "Peace is Our Profession." The slogan first appeared on a sign near a Christmas tree that was outside the Strategic Air Command headquarters at Offutt Air Force Base in Nebraska. An Eighth Air Force public information officer noticed it and it was adopted by a number of Eighth Air Force bases. It was then picked up by the press as the Strategic Air Command (SAC) slogan, causing SAC to actually adopt it. The slogan was discontinued in 1992.

A North American Aviation RB-45C *Tornado*, belonging to the 47th Bomb Group, sits on the ramp at Barksdale Air Force Base, 1949. The straight-wing four-jet bombers departed Barksdale in 1951 with the 91st Reconnaissance Wing, leaving the tarmac to the 301st Bomb Wing, its propeller-driven B-29s, and their tanker cousins, KB-29s. Jets did not rule the Barksdale roost again until 1953, with the arrival of the revolutionary, swept-wing Boeing B-47 *Stratojet*.

While the West Gate of Barksdale was often a beehive of automotive activity, the North Gate was more sedate, giving the air of a country lane. In this sylvan 1950 view, taken less than 20 years after the base opened, the North Gate looks like a view of the future gated communities that would spring up across the country.

In 1950, Old Glory flies proudly in a brisk wind in front of base headquarters, home, at that time, to the command section of the 91st Air Base Group. After 1959, physical control of base property passed from unit commanders to the operational wing commanders.

Built during World War II as Barksdale Field's bus terminal, postwar use of this facility shifted to the Air Police motorcycle patrol. In the 1960s, the motorcycle patrol was disbanded and the building was converted into a local bank branch that operated into the 21st Century.

Boeing KB-29 tankers and B-29 bombers of the 91st Reconnaissance Wing line the Barksdale ramp in 1951, in preparation for transfer to the Far East Air Force for use as reconnaissance aircraft in the Korean conflict. The Wing's B-45s also left in this deployment and never returned.

The 376th Bomb Wing flew the Boeing B-47 *Stratojet*, a medium bomber that incorporated cutting-edge swept-wing technology. More than 1,000 of these aircraft were built, and their takeoffs, often made with the help of rocket canisters, were spectacular and loud. Due to its clean design, extra care had to be exercised maintaining the aircraft. Maintenance personnel in the early years of the B-47 era wore cloth boot covers to avoid scuffing metal surfaces.

In this mid-1950s photo, an unidentified public information officer interviews Hollywood actor Jimmy Stewart, who was then a colonel in the Air Force Reserve. Stewart, a pilot with 35 combat missions in Eighth Air Force B-24s in World War II, visited Barksdale three times to fly with the 301st Bomb Wing. Stewart's real-life reserve pilot training visits to Barksdale greatly increased the realism of his movie, *Strategic Air Command*. (Courtesy Eric Brock.)

Officers of the 376th Air Refueling Squadron pose with a miniature donkey, Fatima, who they acquired and made their unit mascot during one of many "Reflex" deployments. Reflex deployments were large-scale forays that the SAC made to remote bases in such countries as Morocco, Libya, and Turkey to demonstrate the global warfare capabilities of the Air Force.

The donkey Fatima raised a few eyebrows among the brass of the 376th Bomb Wing when she arrived in December 1955, but she proved to be a hit with Barksdale dependents, such as the young girl above, and the local civilian population.

One of Barksdale's notable alumni is comedian George Carlin. He was at Barksdale in the 1950s, assigned to the 376th Bomb Wing's 376th Armament and Electronics Maintenance Squadron. Carlin was probably asked to put zippers on his stripes—he lost rank almost as fast as he achieved it. Off-duty, he worked part-time as a disc jockey at Shreveport radio station KJOE, whose other staffers included Wolfman Jack. As the 1950s came to a close, Carlin's days at Barksdale were numbered. The Air Force was not compatible with airman Carlin's career track, and he was honorably discharged in 1957. But his antics with the 376th Bomb Wing brass provided fodder for his comedy. Local audiences howled with laughter when Carlin performed in the area two decades later and was able to spend an hour telling nothing but Barksdale and area jokes. (Courtesy Airman 3rd Class George Carlin.)

In 1959, Second Air Force maintained its NCO Academy in what would later become the 2d Operations Group headquarters. It was the last original base building used as a barracks and the last of the French Colonial Revival structures to house large groups of service members rather than function as an office complex. Later, Barksdale saw new barracks rise, but they were not as distinctive.

The Douglas C-124A *Globemaster II* transport first flew from the Barksdale runways under the control of the 3rd Strategic Support Squadron from 1953 until 1961. When the 3rd "Triple 3" left, the 917th Troop Carrier Group of the Air Force Reserve at Barksdale took over the job of heavy transport duties. The huge transports, affectionately called "Old Shaky," were less charitably described by some survivors of their flights as "100,000 bolts flying in formation." Still, the reliable airplanes performed yeoman duty, hauling engines, wings, missiles, fire trucks, and pallets of food to deployed military personnel, overseas bases, and victims of floods, hurricanes, and other disasters.

During, and for several years after, the Cuban Missile Crisis of October 1962, Barksdale was home to a reconnaissance unit that flew the Lockheed U-2. Though the unit's presence at the base was a well-kept secret at the time, the airplane had become famous a few years earlier when pilot Francis Gary Powers was shot down over the Soviet Union. Here, pilot Maj. Richard Bouchard poses with his aircraft on the base ramp.

The three key pieces of strategic deterrence enshrined at Barksdale in the early 1960s are pictured here. They include a B-52F *Stratofortress* bomber, an AGM-28 *Hound Dog* missile, and a KC-135A *Stratotanker*. The bomber is part of the 20th Bomb Squadron, while the tanker is from the 913th Air Refueling Squadron. With armed bombers on airborne or ground alert, aided by the tankers, no enemy could strike the United States without paying a terrible price.

Short-range *Nike-Hercules* missiles operated by the U.S. Army's 5th Missile Battalion, 562d Artillery, protected Barksdale in the mid-1960s. Four batteries were planned, but only three were operational by the time the system was phased out, and one of those was a headquarters that had no weapons.

In 1972, Barksdale's 2d Bomb Wing bombers, tankers, and personnel deployed to Andersen Air Force Base on Guam in Operation BULLET SHOT in support of ARC LIGHT missions in the last months of the Vietnam War. Here, family members watch their loved ones leave. One 2d Bomb Wing B-52 was shot down over Hanoi during the LINEBACKER II missions that broke the morale of the North Vietnamese and forced them back to the negotiating table.

In 1976, Barksdale joined the national celebration of the United States Bicentennial through the display of special national colors and the numbers "76" proudly affixed to the castellated water tower. (Courtesy Daniel A. Rigg.)

April 1976 saw the arrival of a special guest, President Gerald R. Ford, seen here with United States congressman Joe D. Waggonner Jr., a major base booster. Ford was one of several United States presidents to visit Barksdale.

In 1978, Barksdale personnel commemorated the base's 45th anniversary with a float for the 1978 Holiday in Dixie parade. The models on the float represent the several eras of aircraft on the base, from the P-12 to the B-52. Personnel on the float are top unit performers, selected for the honor of participation in the parade.

Lt. Col. Hal Rigg and his wife Gerry are pictured here in 1978 at 101 Third Street West, which was later renamed Orville Wright Road. The couple prepares for a day of fishing on one of Barksdale's five lakes. Largemouth bass, bream, and other fish have helped bolster many a meal for Barksdale residents and retirees. Game abounds on East Reservation of the base, which is made up of 20,000 acres of forests, wetlands bird sanctuaries, and natural gas reserves. (Courtesy Arthur C. Rigg.)

In late 1978, a blanket of snow covers Barksdale. The occurrence of snow was unusual enough to cancel school and most other events, and usually led to spates of auto accidents, but the silent white carpet brought out the beauty of the architecture and appointments of Barksdale's stately residences, which had matured gracefully in the 50 years since their creation. (Courtesy George T. Rigg.)

A B-52 crew chief signs the final paperwork stating that a bomber has undergone all needed repairs and is certified for flight. A fleet of B-52s requires thousands of specialists in a variety of fields, from electronics to sheet metal fabrication.

Lt. Gen. Edgar S. Harris Jr., Eighth Air Force commander, delivers the country's first KC-10A *Extender* tanker to Barksdale, March 17, 1981. The jumbo tankers, called Barksdale home until 1994. The KC-10s augment a KC-135 fleet that continues to serve national commitments around the world.

A 1945-vintage B-17G and a replica of a World War II-era Jeep stand guard as the space shuttle *Columbia* and its Boeing 747 mother ship stop at Barksdale for refueling in April 1982. Barksdale is home to a museum of vintage aircraft representing the past of the nation's bomber command, Eighth Air Force.

Distinctive nose art for the KC-10A named "Rollin' out the Red" is unveiled in this photo from January 1987. The airplane, originally named "Lady Luck," was used as a flying ambassador to represent Barksdale and its sibling civilian communities, Shreveport and Bossier City, in appearances and missions throughout the world. Unveiling the nose art are Secretary of the Air Force Pete Aldridge, a graduate of Shreveport's Byrd High School, and Eighth Air Force head Lt. Gen. Kenneth L. Peek Jr.

The service life of "Rollin' out the Red" was tragically short. A fuel pump overheated and ignited fuel vapors during maintenance on September 17, 1987, killing Sgt. Joseph M. Burgio Sr., an aircraft maintenance specialist, destroying the airplane. Then Col. Brett Dula, 2d Bomb Wing commander, took charge of the situation, reassuring the rattled civilian community until it could be shown that an accident, and not sabotage or terrorism, had caused the explosion.

Then Col. Ronald C. Marcotte, today a lieutenant general, led the 2d Bomb Wing during its participation in Operation DESERT SHIELD and DESERT STORM, 1990–1991. The wing's tankers and transports helped create an air bridge of supplies and personnel to the Middle East, while its B-52s deployed to help successfully free oil-rich Kuwait from Iraqi occupation. Seven Barksdale bombers launched the war with "SECRET SQUIRREL," a then-classified nonstop mission to the war zone and back from Barksdale. It remained the longest combat mission in aviation history for more than a decade.

A military spouse and her children solemnly watch the departure of a loved one and other Barksdale friends and neighbors aboard a 2d Bomb Wing KC-10, August 1990. The wing's people and planes would not return until the following spring.

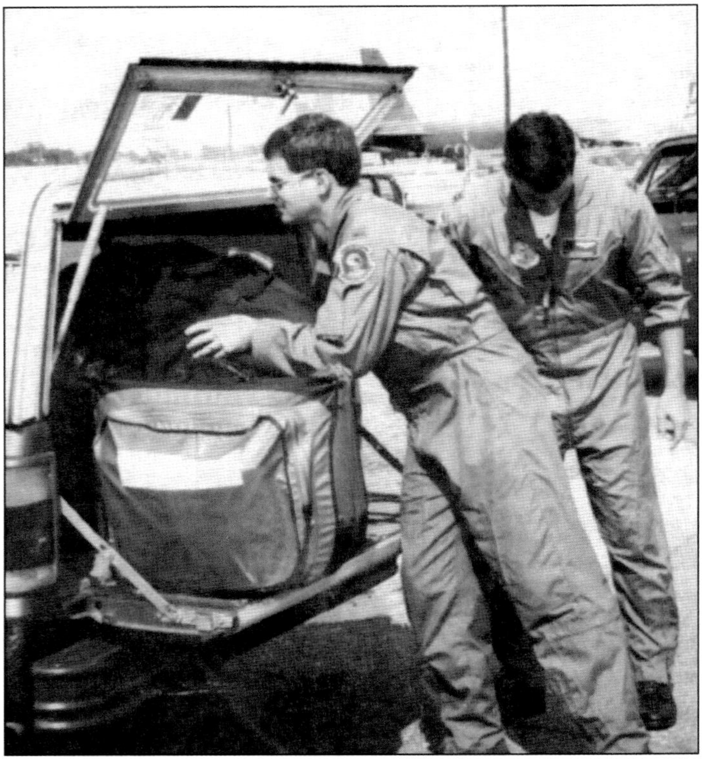

After nearly 35 years of constant ground alerts—and periods of 24-hour airborne alerts—ready crews stow their gear after President George H.W. Bush orders an end of ground alerts in September 1991. To this day, however, light-tipped alert stanchions around Barksdale Air Force Base serve as a reminder of the mission that could have been, and could some day return.

The order that ended ground alerts also eliminated the position of tail-gunner on B-52 bombers. Here, the last tail-gunner in the 2d Bomb Wing is ceremonially "hosed down" in "Fini Flight," a tradition usually accorded pilots.

Seven

A New Era 1992–2001

The Barksdale Air Force Base West Gate has undergone a tremendous transformation from its first days when it was a small guardhouse at the end of what seemed a lonely country road. Reflecting its role as a bridge between the base and community, it was renamed the Shreveport Gate in July 2000. (Courtesy MSgt. Mike Kaplan.)

In early March 1992, two B-52G bombers, one KC-10A tanker, and fifty-eight personnel from the 2d Bomb Wing flew to Dyagilevo Air Base near Ryazan, Russia. The visit, led by Col. James G. Phillips, center, at microphone, marked the first time American bombers had landed in Russia since World War II. The visit would have been unthinkable during the Cold War. The mayor of Ryazan, third from left, and Gen. Maj. Vladimir P. Dovalgo, air base commander, far left, greeted the visitors. Capt. Diane M. Byrne, the pilot of the KC-10A, received much attention, as the Russians no longer had female military pilots. Several girls in native dress were on hand to present bread and salt, a traditional Russian welcome. Byrne is seen below in the center of a group of attentive Russian officers. (Courtesy 2d Bomb Wing History Office.)

In May 1992, two Russian Air Force Tu-95 *Bear* bombers and an An-124 *Condor* transport, along with 58 airmen, paid a reciprocal visit to Barksdale. It was the first time Russian bombers had landed in the United States. The *Bears* and the *Condor* shared the Barksdale ramp with a host of B-52H bombers, including one from the 5th Bomb Wing at Minot Air Force Base, North Dakota. The visit coincided with the annual "Bomb Comp" at Barksdale. (Courtesy 2d Bomb Wing History Office.)

Lt. Col. Michael L. Chase, right, commander of the 62d Bomb Squadron, discusses a Tu-95 *Bear* bomber with Russian Lt. Col. Sergei Folunin at Barksdale. Colonel Folunin landed the first *Bear* bomber on American soil while Colonel Chase landed the first B-52 on Russian soil during the 2d Bomb Wing's visit to Dyagilevo Air Base two months earlier. (Courtesy 2d Bomb Wing History Office.)

After their visit to Barksdale in May 1992, the Russian *Bears* and their support transport left for the long flight back to the motherland. Before they left, they were host to a stream of visitors, including former Air Force captain Dale Brown—now a best-selling author. Brown is no stranger to Barksdale. In 1981, as a navigator on a B-52 crew, he was a participant in the annual Bomb Comp representing the 320th Bomb Wing. (Courtesy Eighth Air Force Museum, Lt. Col. Rod Lees Collection.)

In early August 1994, two 2d Bomb Wing B-52H bombers flew a non-stop around-the-world flight. Taking off from and landing at Barksdale, the aircrews bombed a target range in Kuwait en route. It was the first such mission to include a live weapons drop. It also set new aviation world records for the longest and second longest jet sorties. Brig. Gen. George P. "Peyt" Cole Jr., center left, and then Col. James A. Hawkins, center right, pilots of the two bombers, toast each other with champagne after the flight. Cole, who retired shortly after this final flight, led the mission aboard the B-52 "Laissez le Bons Temps Roulez," which is visible in the background. The name translates to "let the good times roll."

In mid-1995, 2d Lt. Kelly J. Flinn, the first woman B-52 pilot in United States Air Force history, underwent crew training with the Formal Training Unit at Barksdale. She is seen here undergoing training in a simulator with an instructor. After graduation, she was assigned to the 5th Bomb Wing at Minot Air Force Base, North Dakota. (Courtesy 2nd Bomb Wing History Office.)

In mid-October 1996, six Ukrainian Air Force officers visited Barksdale. Team leader Gen. Maj. Leonid Foursa met with 96th Bomb Squadron personnel, commanded by Lt. Col. Floyd L. Carpenter, sixth from the left, in front of the Base Operations building. Brig. Gen. Donald A. Streater, vice commander of Eighth Air Force, stands in center background. (Courtesy 2d Bomb Wing History Office.)

In September 1996, two Barksdale B-52H bombers led by Lt. Col. Floyd L. Carpenter launched Conventional Air-Launched Cruise Missiles against Iraq after it refused to remove troops from its Kurdish-held northern territories. The mission from Andersen Air Force Base, Guam, marked the B-52H's combat debut. The crews received the 1996 Mackay Trophy for the mission. From left to right are Capt. Kelly A. Lawson, Capt. Brett E. Lawless, Capt. James A. Melvin, Capt. Glen J. Caneel, Capt. Gerald L. Hounchell, Capt. Darrel T. Hines, Steven J. Brown (president of the National Aeronautics Association), Capt. Parker W. Northrup III, Colonel Carpenter, Lt. Gen. David L. Vesely, the assistant Air Force Chief of Staff, Capt. John L. Miller, Capt. William F. Simpson Jr., Capt. Grey L. Morgan, Capt. David R. Mack, and Capt. Alan C. Ringe. (Courtesy 2d Bomb Wing History Office.)

In March 1998, Gen. Lt. Mikhail M. Oparin, commander of Russian Air Force Long Range Aviation, and Col. Aleksander V. Demakov, his chief navigator, visited Barksdale. The two took part in a B-52H training mission, the first time Russian Air Force members flew a *Stratofortress*. After landing, the Russians posed with senior personnel and their 11th Bomb Squadron host aircrew. From left to right are Brig. Gen. Andrew W. Smoak (2d Bomb Wing commander), General Oparin, Lt. Gen. Phil Ford (Eighth Air Force commander), Capt. John P. Beck, Col. Demakov, Capt. Andre J. Mouton, Capt. William J. Kilroy, Capt. Richard P. Millard, and Capt. Mark E. Franck. (Courtesy 2d Bomb Wing History Office.)

In 1998, Barksdale's 2d Bomb Wing deployed to the British-owned island of Diego Garcia in the Indian Ocean. It was a response to Iraq flouting United Nations Security Council resolutions. That December, the United States launched a sustained air and missile campaign against Iraq. Barksdale B-52s fired 90 Conventional Air-Launched Cruise Missiles against military targets in Iraq. On December 18, 1998, 1st Lt. Cheryl A. Lamoureux, a 20th Bomb Squadron electronic warfare officer, became the first woman flier in Air Force history to fly a combat mission. She was greeted by Chief Master Sgt. Russell Minor, deployed first sergeant, upon her safe return to Diego Garcia. (Courtesy 2d Bomb Wing History Office.)

In late June 1999, the 2d Bomb Wing's aircraft and crews returned to Barksdale from England after the successful conclusion of Operation ALLIED FORCE. The base fire department was on hand to provide a salute—a good, photogenic hosing-down. (Courtesy 2d Bomb Wing History Office.)

In July 2000, the Second Bomb Wing dedicated its two main gates in honor of the two communities that are its neighbors and supporters, Shreveport and Bossier City. Here the Bossier Gate, previously known as the North Gate, receives its inaugural. Unveiling the new sign, from left to right, are Senior Airman Joshua Pettigrew (2d Security Forces Squadron), Lt. Gen. Thomas J. Keck (Eighth Air Force commander), Bossier City Mayor George Dement, and Brig. Gen. William M. Fraser III (2d Bomb Wing commander). (Courtesy 2d Bomb Wing History Office.)

In July 2000, Gen. Lt. Mikhail M. Oparin (left), commander of Russian Air Force Long Range Aviation, visited Barksdale again, this time with his entire staff. General Keck (right) sports a Russian Air Force camouflage flight suit in the Distinguished Visitor's Lounge at Base Operations. General Oparin points out the words around the Russian national flag with amusement. Capt. First Rank Oleg I. Polyakov (center), an interpreter, explains the wording on the patch, which translates to "Russia—Armed Forces." (Courtesy 2d Bomb Wing History Office.)

A Barksdale Air Force Base security forces member helps form a perimeter as Air Force One prepares to land at the base on September 11, 2001. United States President George W. Bush flew to Barksdale just hours after terrorists hijacked airplanes and crashed them in suicide attacks on the World Trade Center in New York City and the Pentagon in Washington, D.C. Another plane crashed in Pennsylvania after passengers thwarted the hijackers' plot. Within a month, the B-52 behind him would be deployed in attacks against the Taliban and Al-Qaeda. (Courtesy REUTERS 2001/Win McNamee.)

President George W. Bush arrives at Barksdale after flying for two hours following terrorist attacks against New York and Washington, D.C. The president left Florida immediately after a second plane crashed into the World Trade Center, then flew to Barksdale to reassure the nation in a televised broadcast. President Bush then left Barksdale for Offutt Air Force Base, Nebraska. (Courtesy REUTERS 2001/Win McNamee.)

In the wake of terrorist attacks on the nation, President George W. Bush addresses the nation on September 11, 2001, from the Hall of Honor at Eighth Air Force headquarters at Barksdale. The hall honors the 17 Medal of Honor recipients who served with the Eighth in World War II. (Courtesy REUTERS 2001/Win McNamee.)

While President Bush spoke to the nation, security personnel guarded Air Force One. At the same time, two pairs of F-16 *Fighting Falcons* took turns providing a two-plane combat air patrol over Barksdale and the surrounding area. (Courtesy REUTERS 2001/Win McNamee.)

President Bush reassured the grieving nation and stated "the full resources of the federal government are working to assist local authorities to save lives and to help the victims of these attacks. Make no mistake: The United States will hunt down and punish those responsible for these cowardly acts. Our military at home and around the world is on high alert status, and we have taken the necessary security precautions to continue the functions of your government. The resolve of our great nation is being tested. But make no mistake: We will show the world that we will pass this test. God bless." (Courtesy REUTERS 2001/Win McNamee.)

United States President George W. Bush walks with Lt. Gen. Thomas J. Keck, commander of the Eighth Air Force, at Barksdale on September 11, 2001. The general at center, looking at the camera, is Brig. Gen. Bob L. Efferson, Eighth Air Force Mobilization Assistant. Notice the sidearm General Keck is wearing. Security took on a new dimension at Barksdale that day, and remains at a heightened level. (Courtesy REUTERS 2001/Win McNamee.)

Air Force One leaves Barksdale Air Force Base on September 11, 2001, after President George W. Bush made a statement to reassure the American public after terrorist attacks killed thousands in New York City, Washington, D.C., and rural Pennsylvania. The "21" on the tail of the 917th Wing, Air Force Reserve, B-52 above, honors NASCAR driver Elliott Sadler, whose car enjoys Air Force sponsorship. (Courtesy REUTERS 2001/Win McNamee.)

Eight

Preserving the Legacy

Barksdale Air Force Base has been home to many famous organizations and has had many famous and influential people walk its tree-lined boulevards since 1932. The job of preserving those events and activities has fallen to a select few in the Air Force civil engineer squadrons and the Air Force History and Museum Program through the years.

In the late 1980s, part of Barksdale's preservation plan was the demolition of the 1950s quadplexes that had long outlived their usefulness. With the removal of the old "Wherry" housing, the base would once again enjoy the appeal and grandeur of its 1930s-era layout.

With the restoration of the original green spaces, the base property planners and leadership, to better protect the historic integrity of the base, sought nomination to the National Register of Historic Places. In April 1992, some 250 original buildings were placed on the register. Any new construction must adhere to complementary architectural design criteria to be in or near the historic district. The new houses above are examples of new construction built to complement the original housing. (Courtesy 2d Bomb Wing History Office.)

All of Barksdale's facilities undergo periodic maintenance that helps keep the original structures usable and presentable. This maintenance is key to the long-term preservation of the 70-year-old show base and national treasure. Here, a 2d Civil Engineer Squadron painting specialist applies a coat of protective paint on a seven-decade-old officers quarters. (Courtesy Master Sgt. Mike Kaplan.)

From Barksdale's inception, all the varied organizations that have occupied this historic real estate have documented their history. Because military organizations are always moving, those wonderful histories often go with the unit. To provide a sanctuary or repository for the historic property and information about the events associated with the base, a Barksdale Museum was proposed in 1965 by Lt. Gen. David Wade, commander of Second Air Force. He appointed Col. E.Y. Brown as the project officer. Unfortunately, by 1967, a good collection of photographs, a trunk of memorabilia, and the artist concept above is as far as the project got before both men left Barksdale. It would be another decade before the concept of a museum would be revived.

During the fall of 1977, under the leadership of Eighth Air Force commander Lt. Gen. Richard L. Lawson, in cooperation with 2d Bomb Wing commander Col. Ken Patterson, a new museum was planned. This museum would include a collection of historic aircraft, as well as other historic items associated with the organizations that have called Barksdale home. The theme of the museum would be the History of Strategic Bombardment as told through the histories of the 2d Bomb Wing, Eighth Air Force, and Barksdale Air Force Base. Pictured here, from left to right, are the vice commander of Eighth Air Force, Maj. Gen. J.J. Murphy, and Col. Robert Straughan IV, Eighth Air Force Director of Operations and museum project officer. They are about to board the Eighth Air Force Museum's B-17G to fly it to Barksdale as the museum's first historic aircraft.

The Eighth Air Force Museum's second acquisition was this rare Ford-built B-24J *Liberator* recovered from a junk dealer in Tulsa, Oklahoma, in December 1978. The flying hulk made quite an impression on its "flight" to Barksdale. When the old *Lib* was set down on the base tarmac, it marked the first time a B-24 had occupied Barksdale real estate since 1942 when the 44th Bomb Group called the historic field home.

Historic memorabilia that made up a History of Strategic Bombardment display for the 197[illegible] Strategic Air Command Bomb comp was used to seed the new museum located in the 2d Bomb Wing headquarters building. The new museum was officially established in January 1979 as one of twelve Air Force Field Museums under the United States Air Force History and Museum Program. The Eighth Air Force Museum was opened in a ceremony on March 15, 1979.

Barksdale's thousands of acres turn over, from time-to-time, parts of its past to users of its vast reservation. One such example presented itself to a pair of squirrel hunters who happened upon the remains of one of the old Keystone B-6A *Panther* bombers that had been set out on the live bombing and gunnery ranges in the late 1930s. The hunters notified the museum of the find and the staff promptly trekked to the site. After a site survey and photo documentation, the entire tail section of a rare Keystone bomber was recovered. In this August 1980 photo, museum staff member George T. Rigg uses a chain saw to release the hold a tree has from this one-of-a-kind relic from Barksdale's past. The tail section is now on display in the museum. (Courtesy Arthur C. Rigg.)

In formal ceremonies, on June 9, 1982, an international gift from the Royal Air Force, a B.2 *Vulcan* bomber, was presented to the base museum. It would serve as a reminder of the close aviation and diplomatic ties between American and British air forces. The 1950s-era delta-winged bomber was flown from Royal Air Force base at Waddington, United Kingdom, to Barksdale by Air Vice Marshal I.E. Knight, AFC, BA, Royal Air Force. From left to right standing on the platform are Master of Ceremonies Col. James Greer (Eighth Air Force chief of staff), Air Vice Marshal Knight (commander of Number One Bomber Group), and Lt. Gen. Robert T. Herres (Eighth Air Force commander). Knight and Herres have just signed the transfer agreement for the British bomber.

In November 1982, J.J. Murphy, lieutenant general and commander of Fifteenth Air Force, returned to Barksdale bearing a bigger gift for the museum. In 1978, he delivered the museum's B-17. Here, almost five years later, he delivers another Boeing product—a B-52D. This B-52 was the last "D" model in service in the Fifteenth Air Force. At the museum it will tell the story of the B-52 in the Vietnam War. In this photograph, the museum's B-17 and B-24 welcome their bigger and younger brother.

A significant piece of Barksdale history is now on display thanks to the acquisition of this Boeing B-29 Superfortress, of the type that once droned over the skies of the Ark-La-Tex region from 1945 to 1953. Several B-29s were located at an Army munitions testing facility at Aberdeen, Maryland, in 1986. A dozen Barksdale volunteers were sent to dismantle and crate the B-29 above. The tough job was done in just two weeks. With the support of the Military Airlift Command and a colossal C-5 *Galaxy* the old bomber took to the sky one last time on April 17, 1987, shown below. Commander of the 2d Bomb Wing and Barksdale champion, then Col. Brett Dula is seen standing to the right of the recovery team.

Part of the preservation of the legacy of Barksdale Air Force base is to tell the story of the short career of the base namesake—Lt. Hoy Barksdale. Besides staying in contact with the many nieces and nephews of the pioneer aviator, visits to his boyhood home in Mississippi have garnered countless original items that will help document his life. Here, Col. Dave Lay, 2d Bomb Wing Director of Staff, gingerly walks across a mountain of roof and ceiling debris in what was once the family parlor. One item recovered from the parlor was the fireplace facade and mantel, which now complements a replica of the parlor, recreated at the museum.

After the mantel recovery, a vintage field desk, another important Barksdale family artifact, was retrieved. It, too, is part of the Hoy Barksdale Collection at the Eighth Air Force Museum. With the 1860s vintage field desk, or writing station, are Shawn M. Bohannon (left) and Trey Birchfield. It was the team's second and final excursion to the old Barksdale homestead, which is now a ruin. In the photograph below, the Barksdale parlor replica at the Eighth Air Force Museum is seen nearing completion.

Then Technical Sgt. Mike Kaplan applies his knowledge and skill in the restoration of an FB-111 crew module. Kaplan was formally trained as a FB-111 avionics specialist and his expertise proves invaluable in the preservation and presentation of aviation artifacts on display at the Eighth Air Force Museum. (Courtesy Master Sgt. Mike Kaplan.)

Technical Sgt. Bryan Castleberry, chief of museum aircraft maintenance, prepares the Eighth Air Force Museum's P-51D *Mustang* for a temporary display location on base. The museum's P-51 is painted to represent Shreveport ace William Whisner when he served with the 352nd Fighter Group during World War II. The museum provides those who carry on the opportunity to get close to their proud legacy. (Courtesy Master Sgt. Mike Kaplan.)